A Kiss That Never Was:

Poems of Heartbreak & Almost-Love

A Kiss That Never Was:

Poems of Heartbreak & Almost-Love

by

Rudolf Ogoo Okonkwo

© 2025 Rudolf Okonkwo. All rights reserved.
This material may not be reproduced in any form, published,
reprinted, recorded, performed, broadcast,
rewritten or redistributed without
the explicit permission of Rudolf Okonkwo.
All such actions are strictly prohibited by law.

Cover design by Shay Culligan
Cover image by Annie Spratt on Unsplash
Author photo by Sammie Amachree

ISBN: 978-1-63980-828-1

Kelsay Books
502 South 1040 East, A-119
American Fork, Utah 84003
Kelsaybooks.com

to Mukami—
the one who milks the cow

The Look

by Sara Teasdale, 1884–1933

Strephon kissed me in the spring
Robin in the fall,
But Colin only looked at me
And never kissed at all.

Strephon's kiss was lost in jest
Robin's lost in play,
But the kiss in Colin's eyes
Haunts me night and day

Author's Note

There are only two times men express extreme passion: when they are in love, and when they are contemplating suicide. Both require an equal measure of courage, though in opposite directions. The key is that they both spring from the same lake of madness.

He who has known one knows the other. You cannot claim to have truly loved if you have not faced the abyss where everything was on the line. And no one has risked it all like the one ready to surrender everything.

In physical science, the longest line is the distance between the two most extreme points. In emotional science, that same line bends until it becomes a broken circle. A madman looking forward leaps through the hoop like a dancing mantis to become a poet. And a poet who looks backward spins webs like a spider, crawling back into madness.

I am grateful to the spirit that guides the tears as they roll down the cheek, following their centuries-old, well-worn path on faces both young and old, from temperate corners to tropical lands. Sometimes the tears are hot; sometimes, cold. Sometimes, they linger at the edge of the mouth, where the upper and lower lips hook up, tempting the tongue to sneak out and taste them.

Where I was born, on the banks of the Niger, this spirit is called Agwu. You are fortunate if the gods bestow it upon you, but it is essential that you are in harmony with the spirit. If not, doom becomes your name.

In this winter season, it almost took dominion over me. And then I said tufiakwa, and it behaved. For that, and for so much more, I am grateful.

As for the humans who helped to shape this manuscript, I thank Margret Kamau for reading some of these poems in their raw forms, when tears and blood were still dripping. I probably would not have thought they meant anything if Elizabeth Ferris had not read some of them over a decade later and said she saw a pearl hidden in the heap of rock. I'm also grateful to Nimi Wariboko. Your comments on this manuscript were gifts that elicit laughter each time I remember them. Like Jesus turned water into wine, you turned "bearded thing" into "bearded snail." Genius!

—Rudolf Ogoo Okonkwo

Contents

Introduction	17
A Kiss That Never Was	22

OTHER LOVE SONGS

He Died for Me	53
And the Poet Pulled the Trigger	54
Au Revoir, Monsieur Senghor	56
An Elegy for Ola Rotimi	58
A Memo from Death	60
Invitation to Madness	62
Not as We Understand Him	64
Don't Tell Them	65
With God as Our Shrink	66
Search for Peace	67
Our Nursery Is Empty	68
Life	69
Wait, Make I Baff	70
The Witches of Oshodi	71
The Search for God	72
The General and His Jonathan	74
Look at What Pictures?	75
Aba Ngwa	77
I See the Traps They Set for Me	79
Buhari, Your Prick Is Too Small	81
Songs of a Roadside Poet	83

Art by Rudolf Okonkwo

Introduction

How often do you think of me? Yes, you. I think of you often, especially when things aren't going well. I tend to believe that if I were with you, things would be better, maybe even perfect.

Having given up on this life, I think of another. I say, maybe in another life. Perhaps then fate would be kinder to both of us. Please, don't tell me. I know. It's just a way to console myself.

I'm not ashamed to admit this. I'm aware of the eye rolls, the people shaking their heads, as if I've lost my mind. I see them. Serious people. Happily married people. Single people who aren't looking. People whose social media profiles say, "contented." They're in the arms of their soulmates. I'm mindful of those lucky bastards.

I know many of them. Yet their skins glow, their eyes shine, and their hearts flap like butterfly wings when they talk about the one that got away. I've heard them speak—pastors, lawyers, doctors, nurses, drivers, bricklayers, millionaires, and paupers.
Everyone has someone who got away.

Just as DeBarge sings, I know I can't trust my emotions, that when it comes to love, it's often better for the heart not to guide me, because the heart isn't always smart. Still . . .

I know I should know better. But still . . .

As they say in the movies, you got me on the first hello. You gave me something to remember, something profound. It woke something deep inside me.

Dorothy Parker was talking about you and me in her poem "Unfortunate Coincidence." Remember? Do you still recall the lines?

"By the time you swear you're his,
Shivering and sighing,
And he vows his passion is
Infinite, undying—
Lady, make a note of this:
One of you is lying."

Looking back, I wonder which of us was lying. It wasn't me. It still isn't me, because I'm not lying—now, or then.

But I understand. Like all great stories, we faced impediments.

Great stories are about the obstacles life throws our way and the struggle to overcome them. Sadly, we didn't overcome ours.

Or, to be precise, I didn't overcome ours.

So, you transformed overnight into the person I look for in everyone I meet.

There's no deeper sadness than having a part of me still waiting for something I'll never have—the kiss that never was, the hug that didn't last, the wedding that was aborted, the dream knocked off orbit, the unadulterated smile that didn't leave a mark on my heart. Or maybe it did.

If it's easy to let go, then it's nothing from the start. It's easy to say I'd rather be alone than with someone else. But reality demanded I be with someone.

Thank goodness, as Kenny Rogers sings, "there's someone for everyone." Even the rejected end up with someone.

Sometimes it feels like I settled—like I decided to make do with what I could reach. But that's just one of life's curveballs.

These days, I can afford the luxury of thinking we would have been the perfect match. I don't know what it would have been like to face life's challenges with you, or what kind of personality that would have drawn out of you. But I'm sure we would have been the perfect match. I don't know how my emerging personality, the one you didn't get to see, would have affected you. How it might have transformed you and everything I loved about you. But I believe we would have been the perfect match. Even though we were never tested, I still believe.

The heart, after all, is not so smart.

Fate is a cruel party pooper. I said it then. I still say it now. Fate kept us apart. I could have blamed myself, but I think I did all I could. Other than pulling down the sky and splitting heaven in two, I fought for us. I learned to put away my socks. I wrote poems. I bought flowers. I even tried to dance—all to no avail.

I've since become a philosopher, thanks to you.

I now know the worst form of poverty is unrequited love. It leaves emotionally scarred wanderers roaming the landscape of love, robbing and wrecking innocent souls.

I now know relationships are hard. They're hard because we're different, complicated, driven by desires that are uniquely our own. Society demands we relate to others. We don't have to, but the world is structured that way. Whether at work or in life, we confront the need to connect.

The most important relationship we engage in is with our spouses. It's the most complicated negotiation. It calls on us to choose one person out of many with whom to spend the rest of our lives.

Along the way, before we make that choice, we encounter possible options. We face the risk of wanting someone who doesn't want us. It would be unfair if we didn't also experience the opposite—where we don't want those who want us.

But we must choose. And for many of us, we make the ultimate compromise. We choose the best option available.

Now, all I have left are memories. Memory is the soil where new seeds grow from the dying ones. From this soil, new shoots will emerge to sustain the next generation. Next life. Next generation. Next moon. I've come to preach that the "beautiful ones are not yet born."

I've had time to think on this. If you are mine, the one who got away, it follows that I am not yours. Because if I were yours, you wouldn't have gotten away. Am I wrong? Or did you realize too late that I was the one?

You know why the heart isn't so smart? Because when we're somewhere, we long for where we're not. It's human nature. The drudgery of life's realities pales in comparison to the phantom of sky-high fantasies.

They say some ideas are better left as ideas. You're one of them. But honestly, you're more than an idea—you're an ideal. It's the promises of an ideal that make us look forward to tomorrow. Though the truth is, tomorrow is never enough. Tomorrow is just another yesterday on its way.

You're like tomorrow that never comes. And you better not come, because when tomorrow arrives, we'll look ahead to the next tomorrow. The heart's not so smart.

Forget what they say about tomorrow. Forget what my rational heart thinks. In those quiet moments, I find myself saying: only the dead have truly gotten away.

So I ask you again, how often do you think of me? How often do you remember the look? That Sara-Teasdale-look. That kiss that never was.

This entire book could have been called A Long Suicide Note, and everyone would glance at it sympathetically, mutter "poor fellow," and go on with their lives.

But I refuse to give you that relief. That's not a poet's job. It's what entertainers do. The poet's job is to bottle up your heart and shake it until every last drop of bile comes out.

A Kiss That Never Was

I sing America, too. I sing, but not for the same reason
Whitman and Hughes did.
I sing America only because I found Zp here—
Conceived as a dream at the banks of the Niger,
Searched for, like an ant hole for masquerades.
Thousands of miles from home, I found
An African queen, stroking snow, preparing for her reign.
I sing Zp. I'm the Nigerian brother
Who was in a trance when the hustling began.
I came out, left with just a place by the window,
From where I peeped in and marveled at the gem she was.
I had been out there kicking my feet, singing my song,
Nodding my head for Zp, the guest for the feast of Norfolk.
Some days, she winked at me. Some days, she waved.
And someday, she rolled by me like a ghost.
I pride myself on this: I, too, sing Zp.

I followed Njoroge, a college friend, to the airport
To welcome Zp to Norfolk, Virginia.
I was the cool-headed driver.
I had no idea who she was—
Kipchoge Keino's niece—or what I did not know.
My mission was simple: welcome her to Norfolk
And drive her to the dorms of Norfolk State University.
It all changed when she breezed into the arrival lounge
With plaited hair, long legs, and childlike grace
That woke up an earthquake buried inside me.
I was never the same.
She was an apple-faced girl,
Fresh like the African morning.

She had an orange glow about her that radiated without limits.
Her steps were gentle, like the rolling hills of the Uasin Gishu
    Plateau.
If her giggles had not seduced me, her inviting lips would have.
She reminded me of Mukami, my penfriend from Kenya.
She spoke Swahili in a musical tone, like honey to the ear.
She woke up in me all my attachments to Kenya,
An attraction that began after I read Ngugi's Weep Not Child.
She became my Mwihaki.
She was my soul sister.
She had a pen pal in Nigeria. I had one in Kenya.
Her penfriend, Uwalaka, was killed in Lagos, Nigeria,
By street urchins called Area Boys—
Caught in the crossfire in the battle for Lagos
Between the local Yoruba boys,
Who felt they owned the city,
And the numerous ethnic groups, like Uwalaka's Igbo,
Who came to settle there.
I lost touch with Mukami when I could no longer afford stamps,
A victim of the tariff increase.
I transferred my adoration for Mukami to Zp.
How I did it, I do not know.
Despite our shared love for other cultures,
My thirst for water encountered a stone river.

"One day," Zp shrugged, "you gonna walk into my own house,
And I'm gonna have a beautiful white silk gown.
You will sit down and say, 'Where is he . . .?'
And I'm gonna draw you to myself.
And you'll look around, wondering, as always, 'Is it okay if . . .?'"

She paused and lifted her head toward a huge dressing mirror beside her bed.
Her freshly washed hair shined like candlelight.
Within the moonless nights of Eldoret, she would have been swamped.
"And I'm gonna give you a tender hug," she continued,
"For all the days we couldn't see. And the entire rap you took for me."
She took Uwalaka's picture from the dresser
And brought it to her face.
She wanted to kiss it but decided against it.
She laid it back on the desk like an ancient fossil.
"While I sit down on your lap," she said,
"You will go on, 'How are you . . .?'
While I'm playing with your naïve chin, running my hands down your shoulders,
You'll say in a false Kenyan accent, 'Hakuna matata . . .'"
She kissed the picture, her red lips covering his face.
"And I will come for your lips, hungry as a Sudanese vegetarian.
Then you will notice I can't stop.
And knowing you, you'll just say, 'Zp, am I shy?'"
Before her shadow told her to rest,
Before her teeth cut her tongue,
Zp was ready to dance.
But she got pinched by fate and fled.
She fled to find answers to her song.

I failed.
Men fail regularly.
But heavens roar when a man—almost a genius—fails.

It is worse when he fails with an idea nearly a wonder.
I did almost everything to show Ziporah that I loved her.
Tattooed her pet name, Zp, on my marshmallow heart,
Chiseled sonnets dedicated to her on mountain rocks
At the entrance to Norfolk, Virginia,
Beside the sign that says, "Virginia is for Lovers."

I also played Harp for her to the delight of nightingales.
I liked Zp because she aroused my veins like a pot of fresh palm wine.
Despite my difficulty reaching her, her charm—arresting like the specter of *mamiwata*—kept me desiring her.
In her voice, I heard the language of dreams.
In her palm, I saw the road to tomorrow.
For a long time, I staggered like a drunk along winding roads of love by the sea.
In this web of stones and sands, I yearned for a miracle.
Faithfully, I followed the smell of pine needles.
I let a lullaby from palm trees guide me.
Since I discovered her, my soul had been warm like spring dew.
My heart had been lit by an eternal flame as I gently strolled into the holies of heaven.
In life, we close our eyes and dip into the big dipper.
Some come up with stars; others with clouds.
I came up with Queen Zp.
Jealous were lilies over the curl of her lips.
Shy were peacocks who shared catwalks with her.
Pyramids, as wonders, were less amazing than her.
Watermelon, as sweet, was less succulent.
Pictures froze the history of yawns I called yesterday.

Her coming begot seasons of bliss.
Inside Cupid's truck were bars of gold.
Morning papers missed this story of Zp and me
Because editors were busy awaiting the sound of the mating horn.
_____

We danced once—Zp and I.
We danced.
Like two leaves caught in a whirlwind,
We gyrated and twirled.
In her presence, music wooed my feet.
In screaming steps, slowing, quickening, stopping, changing,
I drowned in the soft caress of my sweltering heart.
As boiling sweat tickled down my spine, I rolled my hips.
A luscious aroma teased my rapturous face.
Looking into her eyes released spontaneous laughter into my soul.
Small talks, and I was lost in the spell of her accent.
Each whisper emits flavor of a sizzling steak on a red-hot grill.
We held hands.
Then a warm embrace—like two half-moons becoming one,
Full like an endowed bride's bosom.
After that, each time I heard distant drums, trumpets, and harmony,
I thought of hot baths and streams of desires.
_____

Yesterday, I went to the African Center days after she had gone.
I searched for her shadow and the scent she left behind.
I spoke to the walls, invoking her presence.
Her perfect swinging body, luring dancing feet,
And charming, smiling face failed to appear.
I bent down on the dancing floor, looking for her footsteps.

Listening to the whispering ceiling, I waited to hear her voice.
People beamed around me, but it still felt like I was alone.
Music played like it did last week, recalling my first dance—
A dance I had with her.
She was open to a last dance, but I wanted to dance forever.

For the sake of a boyfriend who, if not for the sex, did not deserve her,
Zp declared me an enemy of the state.
My opinion, I must say.
Something needed to happen to me, something that would change my gloomy mood.
Inside me was a hole the world did not see.
It was the reason why I acted so crudely.
I lost my mind in an unending feud.
All that was left was a soul on the rock.
"Prayers take too long to work," I said.
"I won't be around when my answers come."
"I've tried Prozac, but still, I suck,"
I continued, rubbing my fingers across my tired face.
"I'm not in control of what I have become.
I want to care again. I want to give a damn.
I want to dream and be sane.
I want something to get my nerves calm.
For anything other than this pain, I'm ready to give an arm."
I peeped at my slim arm and wondered who would want it.
In a world of pumped muscles, hollow brains, and fleeting focus,
Who would perch on a timeless Iroko tree?
"I don't wanna hurt myself," I said.
"I don't wanna hurt anyone.

But those are the options on my shelf.
For life has folded my sun."
Off the record, my psychiatrist said I needed to be laid.
I wished Zp would rescue me and make me feel a little tender.
I wished she could be kind and stop me from surrendering to my mind.
But she was busy with someone—Uwalaka's substitute—my reflection.

I tried to find Uwalaka as a way to reach Zp.
If Uwalaka could speak, he would confess a blunder.
He was prompt at the exorcism.
With too much introspection, he almost lost his indignation.
Yet it added no therapeutic value to our deranged minds.
But he could not because he swallowed the phlegm of the gods.
We are delighted by our loot, exhausted by our hate,
And happy that the veil lets us fake happiness.
Our hearts can hold so much and recall so little.
If our destination is doomed, does the brand of car that will take us there matter?
Illogically driven, we bewilder those who search beyond nothing.
For really, nothing is what we pursue.
Our only limitation is the realization that at the very end, we shall be last.
What could be higher than us? Take a good look and say it.
Nothing!

Leisure comes naturally. Quarrel is the habit of the biased.
In our happiness, you find your exhaustion.

She pities the human bondage of our malice.
Isn't it one nightmare we can do without?
Please, give us men with kind hearts and strong nerves.
We have seen enough men with mean hearts and strong nerves,
And too few of those with kind hearts and weak nerves.
The poets call us scum because we acquire money for keeps.
But we have to have money to advertise our poverty.
We relax with trifles.
In our testimony lies the truth about our presumptions.
We made our cage.
Give us Paradise Lost for fun.
Watch us read it with careless abandon.
Have you ever tortured someone before?
No joy surpasses it.
We watch them yell, scream, and bleed.
We watch their skin tear into pieces, their blood gush out like a frightened flood.
We are tickled by the sound of their bones cracking.
It is a wonder—what we are.
A good smack will lead him to our thirsty stream.
We approach reformation; he proclaims redemption.
We climb the rapture ladder; he slides into quiet insanity.
What a pity he has not read the new book
That explained why men have nipples
And why legal abortion reduced crime.
The vicissitude of human fate is often trajectory.
In our world so inverted, hardship endured magnets luxury unearned.
In words and actions, we cheat and lie.
But for his sanctimonious self,
He cheats in his silence.

The day following our expiration, history can eat us for all we care.
Do you want us to care about history?
Has he looked around at the theatre where we perform?
Look very closely and observe the empty seats.
They were reserved for history.
History has since left the building.
He affirmed it each day because he knew what to expect from us.
All we do is validate.
What other deductions was he making?
We have an entrenched resentment for compassion.
Our love is impossible to teach.
O men, where is his Biafran currency? Where?
Our conclusion is simple:
He tells the truth about us; we tell lies about him.
And with God as our shrink, we both cover our faces with shame.
The owl cried the day Uwalaka died.

Zp's cheek trembled as she read it.
What do you call someone who shares no bed with you
But shares a heartbeat?
What do you call someone who lives miles and miles away
But hears your faint whispers?
What do you call a butterfly
That flies across your gloomy sky just when the sun's fins fold?
What do you call a smile
That creeps onto your face moments after life is switched off?
What do you call raindrops
That fall onto your blue basket and stay and stay for you?
What do you call the river
That leaves its winding path and comes uphill to say hi?

What do you call the rose,
Enviously uprooted again and again, still growing back brighter than ever?
What do you call a rainbow
That leaves home quickly enough to hover above you after the rain?
What do you call an eye
That sees the backyard of your soul even in the darkest of nights?
What do you call a hand
That dives across violent waves to catch a teardrop before it hits the ground?
What do you call a princess
Who is not waiting to be rescued by you but will kiss you whenever you meet?
What do you call someone who makes you come alive
The second you think of her like that?
What name is fitting?
What name is soothing if not Zp?

She made me feel so antique with her sleek little charm.
It was the bottom of winter, but I was sweating.
I stood on Nandi Hills peak just for her to hold my arm.
My heart was no sprinter. I was still here, betting.
I raced across many a creek like it was my last grand slam.
At her feet, my legs fluttered on her knees. I was begging.
"Your aura is so scrumptious," I wept.
"Your body is so delicious.
You melt down my muscles.
You left my veins in tussles."
I closed my eyes in anticipation.

My lips coiled in sensation, waiting for a tender embrace,
An end to my long chase.
That kiss that never was because she looked away—
Still haunts me and will haunt me forever.
What she had was so unique, like pink vanilla jam.
"We are smothering to the altar," I said.
"There can be no stopping."
That night, I dreamt of her father giving me a small red snuff box.

Before she was a spirit, I told the moon of her.
Before she was formed, I chose her out of the cosmic bat.
Before she was here, I had been waiting for her.
That was the miracle of Zp and me.
She emerged from the vault of her ancestors
On feathers of floating suns,
A witness to mountains long gone.
Streams of souls soaked in ethereal light
Were carried by a sandstorm of emotion,
Proclaiming love baked in cathedrals of heaven.
From the tickled lips of the poet
Came the unsaid truth of rivers.
Broken dreams reconnect when a little smile glows—
And glows, and glows—
Holding the sky up above
While stretching the earth below.
If I had a rainbow, I would wrap it around her.
If I had a star, I would crown her queen of my world.
On a playground of fate, the festival of dreams continued.
I was astonished that she was still pleased with me.
If I hadn't celebrated her, it must have been because

I remained a cub poet.
She asked why it was this way.
It was because love begins with her.
Blessed is the path through which eternal love travels.
I had thought of paying her for the breast, the burp, and the
    bullwhip.
But gold in quantum wasn't enough.
"So, remember the asterisk," I said.
"It stands for all the things yet to come."
Little did I know that the frowning frogs
Could stop the cows from drinking from the pool.

Firstly, they killed Uwalaka because they had to kill somebody
    anyway.
So they killed him because he happened to be somebody.
But that wasn't his sin.
Secondly, they killed him because he was at the right place
When it was time to kill.
So they killed him.
Still, that wasn't his sin.
Thirdly, they killed him because he was ripe enough to be killed.
With a body so tender, they found his meat irresistible.
But that wasn't his sin.
Okay, let us see. They probably killed him because he reminded
    them of themselves:
Dirty. Rotten. Stinking. Dead.

Willpower is helpless when imprisoned by love.
Love is an addiction like no other.

I knew this the day I met Zp.
Like all pretty things out there, she belonged to someone else.
I understood what that meant,
But no matter how I tried, I found myself hooked on her.
I wanted to be a good boy—not crazy, just doing what was right.
But love was like uranium: stable and safe when untouched,
But forever radiating once cracked.
I wiped off her footsteps from my heart.
I deleted her phone number from my cell.
I keyed her email to my spam folder.
But the faint whispers of her heart still filtered through into my ears.
In the silence of the night, my mind wandered into the field.
Beside the stars in the sky, I saw her eyes looking down at me,
Finally saying, "I love you."
The other day, I went to a dance,
But my best steps wouldn't show,
For they continued to cling to her feet.
Someone daring tried to kiss me,
But my nectar wouldn't flow,
For it was glued to her.
When butterflies passed, I wondered if they carried her message for me.
In each raindrop on the roof, I heard the song of her homecoming.
I looked in the mirror and said those Twelve-Step words:
"I used to love you.
Now, I accept it is unhealthy because you belong to someone else.
I must move on."
Hardly had I finished repeating myself
When the sweet smell of her wrist enveloped me like a fluffy cloud.

Willpower is helpless when imprisoned by love.

"I'm the shit that happened," I told myself.
She was glad to be away from me,
A bad memory of unfulfilled dreams and shattered expectations.
Thahu!
I understand.
"I'm the shit that happened,"
A reminder of things detested,
A dry laughter of a wilting tree growing on a poisoned hill.
Ngwiko!
I understand.
In her heart lived a world conditioned to sing her song.
Anything different, she disposed of.
The oracle wants to tell her this:
The sun will never bow to her whims.
For anything she throws away, the gods will hold her in debt
For hurting one of their own.
As stupid as this might sound, it's the truth:
Eternal is.
"I'm the shit that happened," I repeated.
A gift from her fathers, disguised as hard work.
She failed.
I wouldn't like to judge.
But I could see the command had been aborted.
I don't care what priestess she is,
Or in what shrine she lays her feet.
This is the message from my fathers:
"Your righteousness is a ruse.
Your prayers amount to nothing.

If you keep on hurting, keep on fighting, keep on fussing—
In the name of gods who are loving."
Wherever she might go, peace of mind
Can only come when she drops her current armor
And switches to healing, comforting, and lending a helping hand.
"You can ignore this if you like, but my job is really done,"
I concluded.
"Another reason to ignore this: I'm the shit that happened."

Zp shall start with carrots. This salad is cooked.
Why? She doesn't know.
A language she sings, they call songs.
Where is the sound mind?
A moth could pass for a butterfly if decorated.
But no. On it, the artist wastes no paint.
Last night, she watched an athlete return his medal.
She cried. If only he knew how much she wanted it.
Sometimes, the affluent see no difference between diamonds and
   shoes.
She was once so promising.
Now, she thinks of nothing but love and platitude.
She knows that man and Superman
Have pasteurized everything: truth as jokes and hope as dreams.
She hasn't noticed a difference apart from a snap.
Nothing is more dangerous than a whole lot of knowledge.
Along the valley of darkness, an angel stands by,
Ready to guide its own.
She will evolve.
She will come to me.

All dramas end as soon as the drama king understands
That, at the other end,
His audience sees his drama as mere comedy
While he is pulling his heart out
And drawing petals and shadows with his blood.
Nothing kills drama like that.
And when drama dies, the drama king goes out of his job.
As for the audience, she finds a new theater and a new show.
I, the drama king, hoped to find a new script and a new role to
    play.
However, scripts are hard to get in Hollywood after a certain age.
I retired prematurely, sat at home,
And remembered the good old days when I played on Broadway.
I took solace in knowing that, even though I was seen as a clown
    on stage,
I was faithful to my calling and my heart.
I smiled only when I recalled the line
That all women crave to be desired
Even by those who do not deserve them.

I am an obsolete baby, sucking on your breast.
On it, my life solely depends.
But you've got another baby.
You've got this cute boy close to your heart.
Though you never said it, you want me to grow up.
You want to wean me off your breast.
I am so used to being in your arms, sucking, that I fear to go.
But I have to go.
And he is fighting for his place.
And I know it is his rightful place, for I have had my time.

Or was it my time?
Was it just a fantasy of a baby who is addicted to you?
I may not have grown all these years, but I have had time.
I will take my mouth off your breast before you smack me.
Though a part of me wants you to smack me.
I want to crawl away crying.
You never said you loved me.
I just believed it because I am addicted to you.
You never told me before, but I know I am adopted.
That is why I am not real.
Not the one to be that loved.
I know that whatever I do, I will remain a toy
That comes in when the boy is away.
Though it will cause me pain, I do agree with you.
I need to be weaned off your breast.
Please help. Pick up a dagger, and I will fall onto it.
It is sad to know that for all I dreamt of, death comes as the end.
And the owl cried. This time for me.

What a beautiful dream, sings grandpa Armstrong.
I see dismissed smiles and incomplete kisses.
I see them waking from yesterday's ashes.
And I think to myself, what a lovely dream.
I see healing hearts and rekindling veins.
I see memories falling like sweet summer rains.
And I think to myself, what a beautiful dream.
The winks of sunlight, claps of red roses.
The flag of love rising in the sky—for you, it glows.
I see butterflies flapping wings, humming "I love you."
Oh, that wonderful world is actual.

I hear the chariot's steps; fairytales return.
I'm back to being prince for you, my queen.
And I think to myself, what a beautiful dream.
Yes, I think to myself, what a beautiful dream.
Oh, yeah, Zp.

After a fourteen-year sojourn abroad, Zp prepared to visit home.
She called me.
I had already heard that she was going home.
The same home we were to go to together.
Like Mickey and Saje.
Saje, that son of a gun, stole my dream.
I greeted her call with a threat.
"If you had not called, I would have stopped talking to you.
 Forever.
Forever," I said.
It was an empty threat.
But she was ready for it.
"Please do. Maybe you really should."
Where love rules, people always cry.
Where sniffles end, smiles begin.
It is okay to be unattainable.
But to be irreplaceable—that is deeply unfair.
To have a fascinating story, you have to first pass through the shit.
It is when you pass through the shit and survive
That you can be admitted into the home of legends.
Zp was reflective. She was contemplative.
She was in another place.
It happens when one prepares to go home.
You first go to those places you have been since you left home.

You pick up after yourself.
In some places, you wipe off your footprints.
At others, you shine your words buried deep in marble.

Zp talked about Prancis at home, still thinking about what could have been.
I do not blame him.
With her, you often forget that no is an answer, too.
She chips away at your heart from the moment you behold her.
The moon comes so close every night that it raises your hope
That she can be half as much into you as you are into her.
At night, a tap of an angel wakes you up.
Now you know for sure that eventually, she will come to you.
"How would our meeting be?" she wondered.
Awkward.
"Time and distance have wrecked the path once treaded by passion.
He would be in awe when he sees you.
We all have to accept reality as it is. He will too."
"I don't like this new you," she said.
"I want the old Udol back."
"What has the old Udol done for me?" I asked.
I told her I recently read the old diaries.
"I could not relate to that old Udol," I said.
"I felt like apologizing to all those he came in contact with."
Even the Diary of a Wasted Poet, now called the Diary of the Last African Virgin,
Was disgusting to read. But I could not take it back.
It was the reality of the day.

"Guess what I found recently?" she asked.
"My letters to Hohan."
I knew that because I just read a copy recently.
I read the one where I said she was the civilization we were fighting for.
Yes. I said it.
"When last did you talk to him?" I asked.
"It had been a while," she said.
The last time I guessed correctly was when Sags asked me over AOL chat
To guess who he was dating. I wasted no time in saying it was her.
Everyone wanted her.
And everyone would be proud to have her by their side.
She did not let me finish.
She dropped the bomb.
"If you had kissed me that day before you left for Boston,
Our story would have been different," she said.
I have heard everything, but not this one.
I had always thought I scared her with love.
It was too unreal.
"What will you do if we meet now?" she asked.
"Will you kiss me and get it out of your system?"
"I don't know. I cannot tell," I said.
I could be bold, but I did not want to go there.
I was in public and in my car.
It was not dark yet.
I could not go there. Not with her on the phone.
It would be too quick.
So I told the story.
How it took years to go from Unoma to her.
How she became the epitome of all that had been buried for ages.

I told her I could not love anyone the way I loved her.
"I have to get off this phone," she said.
Zp was saying too much, she thought.
It was always her fear.
Mine was writing too much instead of talking.
She was afraid of being vulnerable.
But you have to make yourself vulnerable so the shy can enter.
Vulnerability is like a door—
If it is open, shy people who do not try outdoors can enter.
But if it is closed, they are locked out.
She was loaded with ammunition.
Yes, if I had. It was easy to say it now.
But not then.
Then.
"Can I ask you a personal question?" she triggered.
A wrestling match.
"I know what it is," I answered.
"How could you know what I have in mind?"
"I do."
"So what do I want to ask you?"
"I won't tell."
The wrestling ended in a checkmate.
I agreed to write the question I believed I would be asked.
I wrote it down and folded the paper.
I would answer it if it turned out to be a different question.
If it were the same question, I would still not answer.
I wrote the question down.
And then she asked me:
"Are you a virgin?"
I unfolded the paper and showed it.
It was the same question asked in the same words.

I did not have to answer.
But that was an answer in itself.

I did not ask to be born.
Sliced tongue, shredded brain, and jumping prayers abound,
Advertising an unbearable eternity.
Stupor of romance loiters.
Muffled narratives stuff ears whacked by contradictions,
While an orgy of lamentation floats on the roof of endearment.
I didn't ask to be born at the crotch of the mountain.
I only wanted to flip the sky and behold my regular self.
"Too much information," she said, her voice flustered.
"I feel like I just read about a disease,
And I'm now more afraid of it than when the doctor mentioned it."
"I have to go," she said.
It was too much.
The unknown had taken off its mask.
It had altered the equation.
The values of X and Y had changed.
But too bad—they had crossed the equals sign.

But what about Dallas? Why did she run when I came to visit?
What about Worcester—why did she perform a disappearing act when she visited?
"What about Veronica?" she asked.
"You wrote those things about her. I thought she was your girlfriend."
Yes. Veronica.
I forgot that she typed the placebo effect.

A deflected decoy of a white flag waving in the wind,
"I'm here. I'm interested. I'm ready to surrender."
"Did you mean those things you wrote in the email?" she asked.
"The proposal?"
"Yes."
"Yes," I said.
"Every unvarnished word of it."

I'll let you in on a little secret.
I've got something the world would give anything for.
I've got hope.
Men don't want to be like me.
They want to be me.
My heart is protected by hope.
Acid rain, ultraviolet rays, and sharp winds
All make their touchdowns.
But invisible always is the beauty of my dreams.
I have the tools to break the barriers of man.
I march forward, risking my sanity,
But creating a new picture.
No matter anyone's angle of view,
I am not falling.
I am not staying down, either.
I'm climbing up.
I'm soaring.
I'm heaven-bound.
Again, I borrowed a wing from a butterfly,
On which I would craft a poem for you.
I hired one thousand poets.
But nothing they came up with adds any color to my craving.

I trail the map of your soul.
I surrender to the fragrance of your shadow.
I stroke the silhouette of your breasts.
I climb the mountain in search of the echoes of your melody.
I give the wind two petals to drop on your heels.
The smoke of my cowardice still blinds my sun every day,
Rolls my moon off the sky,
And drowns each new star deep inside the ocean womb.
Behind my fluttering eyelids are the fires of heaven.
My ashes are coming together, one speck at a time.
The dead are being born again.
And when he is, he will sing through me. Again.
And for you.

I won't let you wait any longer.
Here is my final answer:
It is not a song, my dear,
If it swells me up with oxytocin.
I'm not supposed to sing a sermon,
Even though I'm on my knees.
I'd rather let the truth out of the cage,
And watch the rainbow dance in the sky.
Sometimes, when we talk,
The electricity is too much.
I want to fall into its whirl,
And swim.
I will love you till I die.
Forever and ever is my turn.
I will love you by and by.
That's why I was born.

The thing around my neck—
It won't go down my throat.
Can I borrow your virus
To loosen up my veins?
Please tell me a riddle,
I want to catch my breath.
Twenty years is long enough
To keep a thirst alive.
I must warn you, my dear,
A drop of wine in my dry mouth
Can cause a giant volcano,
Splashing lava up to heaven's gate.
I'm a musical chair dancer,
Frozen up in mid-air,
Waiting for your hunger
To pull me down by the hair.
I've endured the bonfire beneath me.
Pails of snow have been my stool.
Take your fingers off the vinyl, babe.
Let the music play on, please.
For the first time
I'm crazy enough
To shake the wind-up
And reset a heart's beat.
All these must be true
If it's this euphoric.

Tonight on the train
Through chains o' subway,
It may sound insane
If we are not destiny's prey.

Beyond the Island of Sandals,
Where no crane can reach,
To dredge up scandals
As ordained! Impediment impeach.
No brain can explain,
Despite years of replays,
Even sugarcane profane.
It is not enough to convey.
At the Island of Sandals,
Words long in hiding
Lose power over scandals.
Groundhog Day riding.
Constrains detain.
Hauled away to the ashtray,
Hanging sneeze—regain,
Prepaid spot-on foreplay.
Wow! Island of Sandals,
So you're not so far away.
What an urbane scandal
If I stray from what I want to say.
Cuddle my hurricane,
Swallow my cliché as an entrée.
Today, I bury the mundane
For freeway horseplay.
On the Island of Sandals,
There is no figure of speech,
No scandal—
Man, screech and screech and screech.

I have a place in the Canyon of Lovers because I met you.
It is a stool far from the throne.
But it says to the world, bold, in black and white:
I did not come to you by chance.
I ran the race, holding on to my covers and skipping your cue.
Before school, veins are blue as thorns.
But for those called, stories can only be correct:
I did not come to you by chance.
I wipe my face.
This shame is not for others.
Only a chosen few got to play fool for life's roving drones.
These tears so walled can put on no fight:
I did not come to you by chance.
Time is my ace. From him, I take orders.
Due are my dews for me to cool.
Long have I flown to be hauled when a happy ending is in sight:
I did not come to you by chance.

I got a rain check yesterday.
It is for a kiss that will get that one kiss out of my system.
I don't know when I will cash the check.
It may be when my hair is gray or in my next life.
But I can wait, even if it's longer than I have already waited.
It used to be a debt for a dance once lost in a rampage.
It has been upgraded to a kiss—the one that has haunted me since that Friday in January.
It is for my loyalty to love unreturned.
Tomorrow knows I am coming for him.
In his warehouse is my kiss, paid for after years in layaway.

I will claim my kiss, even though God knows it's my love that I
    want.
All stories end when reversal ceases.
In this story, I can picture a reversal.
It comes right after the kiss.
_____

What a paragon of death I am.

OTHER LOVE SONGS

He Died for Me

For Bruce Mayrock, a 20-year-old Columbia University student who, on May 29, 1969, set himself on fire in front of the United Nations building in New York City to protest genocide in Biafra. He died the next day, May 30, 1969.

He died for me.
Like so many others,
He could have asked,
"What concerns me?"
But he didn't.
A distended abdomen moved him—
The bellies of Biafran children,
Swollen with *kwashiorkor*
And our indifference.
He climbed down from his Ivy League chair,
Into the valley of the United Nations.
He wrote on a large cardboard sign:
"You must stop the genocide, please."
But nobody listened.
Nobody stopped.
Nobody paused
To hear the cries of Biafra's children.
If I had been born months earlier,
If I had been weaned from my mother's breasts,
I could have been one of those children
Whose pictures shamed the covers of LIFE.
He died for me.
He didn't have to.
But he did.
Because nobody listened.
And nobody is listening, even now.

And the Poet Pulled the Trigger

for Dubem Okafor

I met him at the Okigbo Conference,
And with Okigbo,
It was all about dirge-puncturing beauty.
We stayed at the same hotel,
Somewhere on the South Shore.
And each evening, after events at Harvard,
We returned to the hotel to drink and yarn.
He came with his wife and children—
A beautiful family encased in a frame.
In my other life,
I painted Saving Mama Udoka.
It was a picture of hidden pain.
Since then,
I have been on the lookout
For Mama Udokas.
I smell them from afar.
The moment I saw her,
I knew she was Mama Udoka.
This America *sef!*
What a famished cult it is.
If the poet were at Nsukka,
He'd be counting anthills,
Drinking palm wine
Straight from the tapper's gourd.
But in estrus-loving America,
The bra is just a metaphor
For crushed scrotums.
It did not help—
He was a poet

Before he became a madman.
Though a tiny line exists,
A poet who looks back
Becomes a madman,
Whereas a madman
Who looks forward
Becomes a poet.
Our ancestors scorn suicide
Not because it manifests cowardice,
But because once sanctioned,
It becomes a quick escape
Out of every life's jam.
Something made the poet puke—
It must be something grave.
For a poet to close the door
On reincarnation,
And look Idemili in the eye,
And say, "fuck you,"
It must be something depressing.

NOTE: Before this news break, Rudolf Ogoo Okonkwo was writing a novel in which the gods cornered a poet and pushed him off the mountain. It started with the sentence, "It helped that he was a poet before he became a madman." He has since scratched the line.

Au Revoir, Monsieur Senghor

With pride, I sing for you, Senghor.
You are now one of my ancestors.
Your spirit has since left Version
For Joal—on a final homecoming.
Today is a day for propitiation,
Not purification.
Your resurrection into eternity
Has made me a myth—
A myth you created
In the lodge of Lycée Louis-le-Grand.
Je t'accompagne.
African priests shall forever pass on
That albino communion you baked.
I speak the dialect of my father,
Yet I am haunted by your blonde negress.
In the armpit of your Négritude,
I am trapped.
Okay, I agree with you—
I am a cultural half-caste.
On my shell,
I have added new cocoons.
But I maintain:
The authentic language of the gods
Is the tongue of my father's incantation—
Not theirs.
Friends, don't call it vernacular
Nor wish to wash it away.
Let them call me pristine—
I do not want to be Africa's Whitman.
I will advertise the hymn
Of our seven rivers and vast forests.

I will not defend the spirits
While building bridges for their devourers.
Where shall black offerings be
In a world civilization?
Académie Française?
Or Académie Africana?
Can I liquidate the Diaspora—
Without you?
Senghor,
You were a trained and acting tortoise.
On the big map of the world,
You scribbled Africa in black and in French.
I appreciate your greatness.
In memory of your essence,
In deference to Hosties Noires,
I shall remain a wild leopard—
Even in the game reserve
I call home.
Au revoir, Monsieur.

An Elegy for Ola Rotimi

I say the gods are to blame.
You say the gods are not to blame.
I say the living have no hope.
You say there is hope for the living dead.
I say what.
You say if.
I say kick the butts.
You say hold talks.
I say our wives are making us crazy.
You say our husband has gone mad again.
I say squeeze the intellectuals.
You say stir the God of Iron.
I say level the field.
You say cast the first stone.
I say, *Ekumeku.*
You say, *Kurunmi.*
I say, *Ogbuefi Ejike.*
You say, *Ovonranwen Nogbaisi* . . .
Now,
I say, what next?
And you say nothing.
I knock on your door,
And you answer not.
I set the stage,
Warm up the actors,
Then call on the director,
And you say nothing.
Haba! You can't do this to me.
Remember, I'm still a baby.
I wash nothing but my stomach.

Baba,
What about man talk, woman talk?
Who will set them up?
Even though you're gone,
And I am the loser,
In maps, manuals, and mambos,
In the woodwork you left behind,
I find hope,
And with hope,
I have everything.
Adieu, my teacher.

A Memo from Death

to Nigerian politicians, their wives, concubines, and cronies

With God as your shrink laureate,
You should've overcome *nju-ofia*.
I can't prop my story anymore,
For I don't think that I exist.
Though my leg is as long as River Niger,
My step is as quick as a wink.
At its climax, I interrupt melodies with dirges.
In my pranks, I hide sonnets in dark laughter.
Just when you say no to *okike,*
I erase your rainbow with my mirth pencil.
I have somewhere else to go,
I always have.
But you are the reason why I'm staying.
On souls under siege
I nurture my nursery
In mortars of lies,
I plant my roots.
In my hunger, I retain
My right to tuck my tummy inside my lace.
In my tears, I restrain.
My wrinkles form channels on my face.
In barrels of dollars, plinth of pounds,
I sink my gimlet tooth.
I have somewhere else to go,
I always have.
But you are the reason why I'm staying.

I am like *Ogbanje*
I come,
I go,

I come again.
But where is my respect?
With clustered prints, I make on your red soil,
Halloween cartoons I draw on your gloomy sky,
Whiplash of wooded pestle,
And monstrous claws of metallic hawks
Knocking down your palm-husk candles.
What else should I do to prove my existence?
I have somewhere else to go,
I always have.
But you are the reason I'm staying.

Invitation to Madness

I have many, many layers.
I learned that when I was still a kid,
When I visited the place
Where emotion accumulates like floodwater.
It builds and builds and builds
Until it takes you with it,
Smashing through fortified brackets
To a place that transcends you,
Making a statement without a period.
It is a brand-new, familiar place,
Made scarier by its need to be secret.
Like a lazy cloud,
It hovers over your head by day.
Like a drunk ghost,
It lurks in the dark by the door.
To escape the nightmare,
A version of you steps out of your head,
Takes a look at you, and gets scared.
It rushes back inside,
Covering you with a blanket of doubt,
On which it is written:
Love is *agwu*
Especially when it is dangerous.
Even when it hurts,
There is a divine purpose why it exists.
Stop being a shadow puppet.
Like a tattoo on the tongue,
The lore of the anonymous
Mocks your shy candle.

But when the status quo ferments,
Myths go naked,
Incarcerating yesterday's deities
For being deficient in dreams.
Superstition doesn't blink—
Else, it sets ablaze
The gown of the last hope.
Take a ride on petals of fire,
For that's what it means to be human.
You don't need an answer
If it is your truth.
If you don't learn something about the world,
You'll learn something about yourself—
And how where you want to go,
Following the path of Thunder's snake,
Is a house of dreams
Built on memories,
With feathers lining the streets.
It invites us to madness.

Not as We Understand Him

Yesterday, I had sex with God,
Right at the porch where the cloud sleeps
And the tides come to get a kiss.
I was sure it wasn't a dream,
For I checked the basement of my brain
Again and again and again.
While others sell their bodies for cheap
And collect rent for keeping silent,
I went for eternal orgasm
And a subscription to Rainbow on-demand.
Come back in nine months,
And see the baby we shall bear.
No, I didn't seduce God.
How could I?
God seduced me.
I resisted.
I played hard to get,
Said I had a girlfriend.
Still, She persisted in Her hunt.
When She caught me,
I jumped out of myself.
She gave me a taste of enchantment,
And I haven't been the same again.
Oh, I forgot to say—
This poem will poison you.
Damn, that should've been the first line.

Don't Tell Them

Please don't tell them
What they have started.
Don't call it by its real name,
Or they might be traumatized.
Don't tell them they must jump
From 10,000 feet
Without a parachute.
Let them think
Hunger and anger took them
To the top of a dwarf mango tree,
Shaking it for ripe fruits.
When they ask why the cock crows,
Tell them they squeezed the toothpaste
Out of its rusting tube.
Wait until tomorrow
To tell them
There is no way
To put the toothpaste back in.
Whatever you do,
Don't tell them
They have started a revolution.

With God as Our Shrink

Correct me if I'm right—
This dance of infidels
Has nothing to do with the curse.
Pirates of the Niger
Grapple at Heaven's gate
With scrotum monologues.
Bad satire, unfinished symphonies—
They dazzle the expectant father.
Immersed in diets of worms,
All our ahas drown.
The sermon in Washington
Went against our *Tufiakwa*.
The audacity of hope—
Crushed by the riddle
Of our last *Ogbanje*.
Goodbye to a wasteland,
The reporter sings.
Welcome our female eunuchs,
Male daughters cheer.
Our funeral is postponed
Until we endorse
The blonde called Nigeria.
With God as our shrink,
It shall be well with us.

Search for Peace

When our world becomes as turbulent as this,
Many keep saying the time is His.
When some people only hiss,
While others passionately kiss,
When a wild wind carries away the bliss,
And every step ends in a miss,
When diseases occupy many stomachs
While from the anus death makes releases,
When nature comes up with a tease,
While the whole world is at unease,
When politicians neglect the "please"
Of millions of lives, putting them on a lease,
I designed a little quiz,
Not meant for lovers of cheese:
What can ever cease
This search for lasting peace?

Our Nursery Is Empty

Our nursery is empty,
Only the sick and the weak reside there now.
Weaning came by force.
Kids' hands were pulled off their mother's breast,
Their mouths sealed to kill their screams,
But their tears drop all through the way,
Diluting the seas across our land.
Our nursery is empty,
After we had been dumped on plantation farms,
Another bunch of fake gardeners besieged our motherland,
Trimming, fertilizing, polluting, and stealing.
It took a wildfire to chase them out,
Leaving nothing but ashes on mined fields.
Our nursery is empty.
Those who survived swallowed the gardeners' bait
And got hooked on guns, loans, and grudges.
These squabbles mean just one thing:
No man with a phallus lives there anymore.
Oh! Our nursery is empty.

Life

Giving commands has always been easy:
Catch the bullet, catch the shrew.
But what about the water to wash our hands?
That is when they come up with saliva.
Old people have lots of rags,
Wrapped together, they look like a ball of wisdom.
I have told my peers more than once:
I can't sit in my room and crush my testicles.
Dad says emergency surpasses the brave,
As if an emergency is not just a test of bravery.
It's not good for the penis;
For this reason, it bows its head.
But if it dies not prematurely,
It will eat that bearded snail.

Wait, Make I Baff

Wait, make I baff
Before dem virgin girls
Return from the stream.
Something dey scratch me for yansh,
E dey pain me like pepper.
No be the *ogbono* soup Amaka cook,
No be Mama Ebuka's pepper soup.
Na something about that woman
Wey dey give her pikin
Two breasts for one mouth.
I no fit siddon dey look—
Wait, make I baff.

The Witches of Oshodi

A bird falls from the sky,
Lands on land,
Turns into a woman . . .
Mere urban legend—
Until the camera phone came to Oshodi.
Bill Gates scratches his head,
Mark Zuckerberg pulls out a calculator.
Oshodi crowd gathers—
"Lynch the woman,
Lynch the witch!" they scream.
Meanwhile, the world pays billions
To watch Spiderman,
High on special effects,
Do the same on a movie screen.
Oshodi, don't just get a life—
Find her a Hollywood agent.
Years of looking at high-tension wires
In Old York City and New York City,
I've never seen Spiderman hanging.
Oshodi, go get the woman an agent, would you?

The Search for God

The search for God
Can be as mysterious as God Himself.
Some go to Mount Carmel to find Him,
Others go to Mount Goat.
But the wise ones
Go to the house of the deep, the deeper, and the deepest.
Some kneel on hollow ground with hands in the air,
Others lie on Dangote cement floors
To hear His footsteps.
Forget the insinuation
That when two or more are gathered in His name,
He will be there.
He favors His tribesmen in Jerusalem,
And those who gather there get served first.
He welcomes the one who drinks Champagne,
But not alcohol.
He embraces the one who hasn't paid his workers for three months—
When they can get filled drinking River Benue.
He cuddles the one Churchill's people banned
For turning His temple into a den of thieves.
And the one South African wind exposed his anus,
He dusts off the dollar stains on his red robe.
He is that merciful to His people.
It is all the fault of the hymns,
Since they proclaimed:
"Jerusalem, my happy home."

Home is no longer where your bed is.
The bottom line is this:
The bottom that won't stay at home
Must have been stung by a vicious termite.

The General and His Jonathan

Why am I thinking of pedigree,
Thoroughbreds, and their likes?
Chubby corruption
That has grown a mustache,
When I should look at the picture
And thank God—
That as He lifted His chosen one,
The one with a lucky name,
So shall He lift me?
Why am I like this?
A roadside poet,
Corner-corner thinker.
Feasting in the bowls of insanity.
A thousand years of ecumenical review
Will never canonize my script.
So, why try?
Why worry?
I'm sorry.
It may be time
To look Rumi in the face
And say to him:
Despite eternity's fall on her knees,
That proposal was just a sham.

Look at What Pictures?

Look at these pictures.
Look hard at them.
These are people—
Nigerian people,
Displaced within their own country.
Again, look at these pictures.
Look hard at them.
Either you were like them,
Or your folks were like them.
If not,
You will be them in no time.
Or, if you prefer,
You could be them in due time.
That's what happens
When we allow injustices to mutate.
Look at these pictures.
If it wasn't you,
If it isn't you,
It could still be you.
That's what happens
When we clone in our hearts
The virus that eats equal rights.
Look at these pictures.
Look hard at them.
Did you see the ghost of yesterday
Hovering over their heads?
Imagine what tomorrow holds—
For them,

For their children,
And the incarnate of the ghost.
And the man
Charged with securing their lives and properties—
He is busy running for re-election.

Aba Ngwa

Even Chernobyl looks livelier.
No, nobody dropped a nuclear bomb here—
Just waste.
Waste of a generation,
Begotten by a ravaged generation.
Not even in Biafra,
With bombs dropping from the sky like rain,
Did these once-proud people
Crawl on their stomachs to lick their own filth.
Oh, but it's their filth.
Not anyone else's.
It's theirs.
Not even T.A. Orji's depraved filth.
Did you notice the vultures wouldn't visit?
Too dirty for those merchants of death.
Yet, they raise our children here,
They toast our girls here,
They guide bitter leaf soup into their mouths,
Right in front of this mountain of filth.
Dirt is your name, Aba.
Dirt is all who call this place home.
You may wear white from head to toe,
Immaculate and conspicuous,
To worship at the Church of the Holy Ghost.
But I tell you, my brother,
I tell you, my sister—
Your soul is as filthy as the walls of the anus.
Your government has failed,

But so have your hands,
And your brains,
And the little things that make you human.

I See the Traps They Set for Me

Yes, let us see if he will ignore this—
This magnificent cement elephant,
Sitting pretty on Uyo's porch.
Let's see what he will say now
About our march
Toward being Dubai on the Niger.
I'm sorry to disappoint you all—
I will not ignore it.
I see it.
I acknowledge it.
And I marvel, too.
I'll visit it in a year.
Then, I will compare the greens in these pictures
With the greens I'll find on the ground.
I will listen to the sound of generators
To see if they are tired of buzzing.
I'll check their record books,
Counting on my fingers
The great events that have taken place there.
I'll check if poverty alleviation money
Has once again been used
To fly Beyoncé in to perform for Jonathan.
Because I care about players on the pitch,
I will look for a nearby emergency room—
A place where a player who breaks his leg
Could be taken in minutes.
I will stay with my brother, who lives nearby.
Hopefully, he will have pipe-borne water by then,
Because the last time I visited him,
Some eight years ago,

When Akpabio was coming in,
He had none.
Then, as we waited for a water tanker
To deliver his drinking water,
He assured me that Akpabio had promised—
That Akpabio would take care of it.
Yes,
I will see if Akpabio took care of the side effects
Of the thirst for European soccer,
Before quenching the thirst for clean drinking water.

Buhari, Your Prick Is Too Small

for Lekki Tollgate massacre victims

If you listen closely,
You will hear whispers—
Somewhere in Nigeria—
Mistaking Buhari for a man.
You might even hear Buhari boasting,
Claiming he could shift wombs,
Though some say he only rocks the cradle.
Nobody dares to tell him:
"Buhari, your prick is too small.
Stick to the nostrils,
Where your mates flex."
Surely, you have heard
What Buhari the terrible
Did to our children in Lekki.
Do not let him claim the credit
For breaking our children—
Our beautiful children,
Poised to plant hibiscus on our land.
Spread these words,
All who encounter them,
And tag with your tears
Trigger-happy Buhari, the terrible.
Before our very eyes,
Buhari relapsed,
Coughing out sorrow,
Stamping on our tomorrow.
He never told us
He was off his medication—
Imported from London.
With a white handkerchief,

He hid the pus
Gushing from his nose.
But we should have known,
Seeing him pick his teeth,
Squeezing out rusty water
Stuck in the middle.
The Hague is calling,
And I bet it won't be hard to catch him.
The smell of gunpowder
Follows him like a shadow.
Forensics will trace him—
His knuckle prints flow
On our bloody lake,
Long after the ripples
Of his punch have dispersed.

Songs of a Roadside Poet

I.

Mystique creeps around their horrendous smile.
Hors concours, the Guardian reports.
No sacramental, no Russophile among them,
Yet the scoreboard pits them against pretenders.
Lyrical is their dipsomania,
Invincible their disposition.
Herbalists all,
Queuing on the Maginot Line.
With depressed phalluses hanging out,
Lymphatic by day,
Supersonic by night.
Phenomenal when the church bell rings,
The prodigals recant and return,
Swelling the party of hallucinators.
Hamburgers push off kwashiorkor,
Keeping life's logarithm balanced.
No one notices,
But the ovoviviparous continue.
One day,
When these caterpillars shed their skin,
Our butterflies will emerge.
Until then,
The owls rule—
From Ketu to Okokomaiko,
From Oshodi to Ojuelegba.

Chorus:

One day in this country,
The tears of hungry masses
Will melt Olumo Rock down.
The fears of suffering commoners
Will dry up the Niger.
The cartoons of trouble roaming about
Will discharge their content like dew.
Then, no one will remember
How we pleaded for care and share.
One day in this country,
The cold hand of Jos will spread out
And freeze the sinners of Lagos.
The encroaching desert of Sokoto
Will leap to Port Harcourt
And turn the Garden City brown.
The visiting seas of our beaches
Will turn back in anger,
Leaving the coastland sandy.
Then we shall look and see
That our black gold is gone—
Gone with its heavenly curse.
Perhaps only then
Shall we regain our sanity?
For now,
Let someone advertise our poverty
To those who love the word liberty,
And stop borrowing foreign insanity
In exchange for our nation's sovereignty.

II.

If not for Nigeria,
I would have been an Oduduwan,
Living in divine peace and joy
In a land where beautiful mornings are within reach.
But I am trapped in the belly of this hippopotamus,
Struggling to rise beyond its knees.
The tradition of my fathers
Is trashed in the parish of their invented trinity.
Our herbs conflict with our tongues,
Our charms are at war with our witches.
When Christmas comes,
There is nothing in the box to open.
I have climbed the rocks of Abeokuta,
Kissed the forests of Ile-Ife,
And seen dreams in this darkness.
That I belong here is only in your memory,
For we have no other dates.
I am getting out of myself,
For there is no other reason to stay.
Together, we have been growing apart.
The man does not know why he needs the woman,
The baby has chosen to ignore its mother's breast.
I am calling it a day.
After all, what use am I
If nobody needs me?

(Chorus)

III.

If not for Nigeria,
I would have been a Biafran.
I would have created a world in my image,
Where fear is cheap, and daring is cool.
From the heart of the Niger,
I would have carved out an empire
From which Africa's sun would rise.
Today, I am an adopted son—
No one fully embraces me.
They eat their burgers, cheese, and fries,
Yet no one will let me eat my fufu and bitter leaf soup.
Amadioha has told me the tortoise's story
And why I must carry my cross.
Mummy told me what my fathers built at Uli,
She taught me the Enyimba song,
And how our masquerades can still invoke the spirits.
I am going to Awka tomorrow.
I am sure, over there, they have the tools
To cut off these shackles around my feet,
For I am eager to fly.

(Chorus)

IV.

If not for Nigeria,
I would have been an Arewan,
Free from the pretense of loving the pastor
And his Sunday school lessons.
I did go back to Queen Amina for inspiration.
If not for Nigeria,
I would have been an Ijawan,
Grilling our fishes in crude oil.
If not for Nigeria,
I would have been a Urhoboan,
Chopping from Oba dem stool.
If not for Nigeria,
I would have been an Igalan,
Restoring dignity to the Benue River.
If not for Nigeria,
I wouldn't have been just another Teletubby.

(Chorus)

About the Author

Rudolf Ogoo Okonkwo is a Nigerian-American journalist, writer, and adjunct professor of Afro-Diaspora Literature and Post-Colonial African History at the School of Visual Arts in New York City.

For fourteen years, he has hosted the Dr. Damages Show on SaharaTV & IrokopostTV online. The satirical show has been featured in *The New York Times, BBC,* and *The Guardian* (London). He is host of 90MinutesAfrica and HaveYourSay247. A regular panelist on The Diaspora Perspective on Voice of the People TV in Nigeria, he writes a column for *Peoples Gazette*.

His books *include This American Life Sef, The Secret Letters of President Donald J. Trump, Age 73,* and *When Trump Met Kamala*. He is also the author of a book of essays, *Children of a Retired God*.

A memoir piece "The Beginning," published in *Crab Orchard Review,* was a finalist in the 2010 John Guyon Literary Nonfiction Prize. His short story, "The Butcher, the Surgeon & Me", was a finalist in Glimmer Train's 2009 Open Fiction Competition.

Okonkwo has been interviewed on NPR and the BBC Africa Service, and his work has appeared in *Quartz, This Is Africa,* and *La Repubblica*.

Okonkwo holds a bachelor's degree in engineering from the Federal University of Technology Akure (Nigeria) and an MFA in Professional and Creative Writing from Western Connecticut State University, USA.

www.ingramcontent.com/pod-product-compliance
Lightning Source LLC
Chambersburg PA
CBHW030910170426
43193CB00009BA/798